William Burdon

An Examination of the Merits and Tendency of the Pursuits of Literature

Part First

William Burdon

An Examination of the Merits and Tendency of the Pursuits of Literature
Part First

ISBN/EAN: 9783337203207

Printed in Europe, USA, Canada, Australia, Japan

Cover: Foto ©Thomas Meinert / pixelio.de

More available books at **www.hansebooks.com**

AN

MIN

OF THE

ITS AND T

OF TH

UITS of LI

R. BROWN,

SOLD BY

DER, LONDO

N AND CO

THE Author has given a quotation in the title-page, which proves two things of ſome conſequence: firſt, that he quotes from memory; and next, that he does not underſtand Greek; for he has forgotten two words in the original, which are in the accuſative caſe, and given two by memory, which are in the dative: τοις εμοις λογοις επινευσατε, inſtead of την βασιλικην κεφαλην επινευσατε. It is moreover to be wiſhed, that the Author had thoroughly read this treatiſe, and imbibed ſome of the mildneſs of its ſpirit: it is the moſt candid, moderate, and intelligible, of all the apologies for Chriſtianity, and of all the writings of the Fathers.

*AVERSE to formal dedications and long prefaces, I will not trespass on my reader's patience with either; and I have but one acknowledgement to make to my learned friends: To the Rev. Hugh Moises, late Master of the Free Grammar-School at Newcastle-upon-Tyne, and late Rector of Graystock, in Cumberland, I am indebted for what I esteem my greatest happiness; from him I first imbibed the love of learning; to him, therefore, I dedicate the first fruits of my classical studies: for nine years of my life, I found in him all that * Quinctilian requires of a schoolmaster, and many others have done the same. —I am happy to have this opportunity of paying a tribute of respect and gratitude to an excellent, but neglected man, for all that I owe him: if he does not now enjoy the reward of his merits, the shame is with those who have never given him, but most with those who have indirectly deprived him of preferment: yet he is rich and happy: his happiness is in his own conscience, and his riches are his good works; these no man can take from him. Tho' he is now in a ripe old age, may he yet see many years of honour and of comfort.*

Sic omni detectus pectora nube
Finem Nestoriæ precor egrediare senectæ.

Statius Syl. 1—3.

* Lib. 2. c. iv.

EXAMINATION,

&c.

TO attempt to examine the whole of a Work, which embraces ſuch a variety of ſubjects as the PURSUITS of LITERATURE, might ſeem a raſh and hardy undertaking, were I not ſatisfied that many of them are treated ſo ſuperficially as to require no great depth of reading, to expoſe to contempt the arrogance of an Author who attempts to guide the Public Taſte, where he ſeems ſo little qualified to decide: But before I enter into a particular diſcuſſion of the merits of the work, let me not omit to expreſs my indignation, with all the force I am maſter of, to reprobate the dark, inſidious, cowardly policy of ſtabbing in the dark, thoſe whom he dares not face in open day. He pretends to be the advocate, the defender, the ſupporter of every thing that is noble and gener-

 ous,

ous, of every thing that is Britiſh, of every thing that is worth preſerving in our national conſtitution and character; and he diſgraces them both, by a conduct worthy only of a ſicarious Italian, without either courage or honeſty. Does he imagine that any man regards the reproofs of an anonymous Cenſor, who ſhews no title to his office, either from his character or his former exertions? Let him look to the great Satiriſts of former times, and ſee how they acted, as he is fond of the authority of the Claſſics: They publicly ſtood forward to attack vice and folly, defended by the triple armour of their own innocence; and whenever they came forth to the charge, they ſpread terror in the ranks of their enemies: They were always dreaded, becauſe they were known. Had Horace, Juvenal, or Pope, concealed their names, their writings could never have outlived themſelves; after a little temporary popularity, they muſt have ſunk, where the Author of the Purſuits of Literature is ſinking, into nameleſs oblivion: But now they and their Authors live together; we admire them for the ſake of each other; the men, becauſe they had the courage to avow them; and the works, becauſe they required

quired it. But however our Author may flatter his own vanity, his Satire carries very little weight with it: Many people read, but few regard him. Does he think that the efficacy of his book will be loſt, if his name were known, and that his only chance to be attended to is to ſneak under the fame of another? Or does he fear the perſonal conſequences of his many perſonal attacks? If ſo, Literature and Morality will not be much benefited by a champion who dares not defend them openly, as they have a right to be defended. The book, it is true, has gone through eight editions; an extraordinary number for a work which is partly literary, and dragged down too by ſuch a dead weight of quotations: But its reſiſtance to theſe diſadvantages is in a great meaſure owing to the political matter it contains, and the number of individuals it attacks; for ſome people have a great deſire to ſee what is ſaid of them in print; and others are not leſs deſirous to ſee what is ſaid of their acquaintance, particularly if it is ill-natured. But let not the Author be proud of this circumſtance; for it is no more a proof of public approbation, than the crowds that attend many public ſights* are a proof that they are liked: There is a great difference between liking, and liking to ſee. Should it be aſked, why I (who am not even alluded to in the book) ſtand forward the champion of other people? I will anſwer, It is not the men, but the principles which are attacked, that I am anxious to defend: If others have not thought the Author worthy of an anſwer, I have; not becauſe he has the talent to be dangerous, but becauſe he has the power to miſrepreſent; not becauſe he is vigorous, but becauſe he is venomous; not becauſe he is admired, but becauſe he is read, and read too by many who cannot ſee faults without having them pointed out. With ſuch intentions I have ventured to come forward to a conteſt, in which I truſt to be in ſome meaſure equal to my antagoniſt; not becauſe I am a David, but becauſe he is no Goliah. I have judged that the beſt method of ſhewing the book in its true light, is to examine it piece by piece: It is the longeſt, but it is the faireſt; and if I ſhould prove, as I truſt to do, that the Author's egotiſm and vanity are every where evident; that his ſtile is poetical and affected;

* An Execution, or a Whipping, for inſtance.

affected; that he is declamatory, and destitute of argument; that neither his quotations, nor his applications of them, are just and honest; that he has not read many of the works which he censures; that his judgments of books and men are not impartial, but directed by his political prejudices and his private dislikes; that his sentiments on politics and religion are illiberal and bigoted; and that he is every where peevish, pedantic, and malignant; that, under pretence of love for our English Constitution, he preaches up despotism, which is the only government he heartily admires; if I should prove all, or even part of this, I trust I have done a little towards shaking his character with the public, and contributed my share to free them from the imperious tyranny of a literary Dictator. An Advertisement prefixed to the eighth edition contains some acknowledgement of the Author's errors; and if he goes on with these confessions, he will at last obtain some degree of credit.

"Yet I am still of opinion, that no man of
" candour and reflection could wish to see
" any mistakes continued without correction,
" or the various parts of it again presented to
" the public, without improvements and additions

" ditions to the poetry and notes, as cir-" cumſtances aroſe to prompt or to require " them." This is a proof that much needs to be, but not that much has been, amended. Let me aſk the Author, *en paſſant*, if it is permitted, by the rules of punctuation, to begin one ſentence with a capital letter before another is finiſhed?

" It will be ſeen, however, that, by omiſ-" ſions and alterations, I have expreſſed a li-" beral concern for my *unintentional* miſtakes, " with the ſpirit and breeding of a gentle-" man." There are other things required of a gentleman, which he has not done, while he has done thoſe things which he ought not to have done: He has yet much ill breeding to atone for. Such is our Author's luſt for quotation, that it is as impoſſible for him to write a page without it, as for a hardened ſnuff-taker to be ten minutes without a pinch. Let me adviſe him, however, always to ſtick to the text, and not, when a paſſage makes directly againſt him, attempt to turn it his own way, as he has done the following from Johnſon's Debates: " The heat which has offended them " is the ardour of conviction, and that zeal

" for

" for the ſervice of my country, which " neither hope nor fear ſhall influence me to " ſuppreſs. I will not ſit unconcerned when " (PUBLIC) LIBERTY is threatened or in" vaded, nor look in ſilence upon *(intended)* " PUBLIC ROBBERY. I will exert my en" deavours, at whatever hazard, to drag the " aggreſſors to juſtice, *whoever may protect* " *them*, AND WHOEVER MAY (ULTIMATE" LY) PARTAKE OF THE (NATIONAL) " PLUNDER." Here, by the help of one alteration, three inſertions, and two omiſſions, he has twiſted the paſſage, or, as he calls it, applied the ſpirit of it to his purpoſe.— This is a new mode of quotation, which, if generally adopted, will be ten times more dangerous than the ravages of criticiſm, for that ſeldom extends beyond a word at a time, but this will in the end pervert the ſentiments of an Author ſo completely, that he may be made to ſpeak any man's opinions but his own; nay, even the moſt oppoſite.—I intend to do the Author a favour which he has no right to expect, but as it is meant for the public, and not for him, I do not aſk his thanks: As his quotations are in general very looſe, ſome without references, ſome with references

ences very infufficient, I will fupply them as far as they are to be fupplied; for many, I fufpect, are of his own making, as he feems fonder of Latin and Greek than his own language: I will at the fame time point out their errors.

"Δία Ευφημίας ϗ δυσφημίας." 2 *Cor.* vi. *ver.* 8. In the motto to the introductory letter he has given a long quotation from Taffo, which, as it ftands, appears to have been taken regularly from the Poet, without any other words intervening; but it is not fo, there are no lefs than two whole ftanzas between them: This licence may be permitted when, as in this cafe, the meaning is not altered; but in other cafes, of which I will give many inftances, it is dangerous, becaufe an Author may be made to fay what he certainly never intended; but though the meaning is evident, the force of its application is not fo eafily feen, unlefs the Author wifhes it to be underftood that he has any thing to do with the powers of the lower regions, to whom the words of the magician are addreffed. In the three firft paragraphs of the introductory letter he feems to glory in his fhame, when he exults in the impoffibility of finding him out: In fpite ſpite of all that he máy ſay to the contrary, I am of opinion that it is not the work of one man: his word will go for nothing, becauſe no man can tell whoſe word it is. He has only one method of diſproving conjectures; till he adopts that, every man's conjecture will have the weight it ſeems to deſerve. If I am not miſtaken, I am juſtified in applying the words of Martial to one of the perſons concerned—

——————Facile eſt Epigrammata belle
Scribere, ſed Librum ſcribere difficile eſt.

Lib. 7. Ep. 84. ad Sabellum vanum Poetam.

I might add too, that it is eaſier to make ſpeeches—the Doctor underſtands me.

"I always thought with Junius, that a "printed paper receives very little conſider- "ation from the moſt reſpectable ſignature; "but I would not be underſtood to inſinuate, "with that great and conſummate writer, "that *my* name would carry any weight "with it." Our Author ſeems here to miſtake the queſtion; it is not whether a book is of more or leſs value with or without a name, but whether it is honeſt for any man to conceal his name from thoſe whom he attacks. The authority of one anonymous Writer can never juſtify another.

" Criticiſms and diſſenting conjectures on
" the ſubject are alike the object of my in-
" effable contempt. More ſagacity muſt be
" exerted than the *Ardelios* of the day are
" maſters of, who are ſo kind as to think of
" me, who moſt certainly never think of
" them. It is however my reſolution, that
" not one of theſe idle conjectures ſhall ever
" be extended to *you*. '*Quid de me alii loquan-*
" *tur, ipſi videant; ſed loquentur tamen.*'* It is
" a voice; nothing more. Prudence indeed
" ſuggeſts a caution which I unwillingly
" adopt, and reſtrains the eagerneſs I feel for
" the diſplay of *your* virtues and of *your* ta-
" lents. But thoſe virtues muſt at preſent be
" left to the teſtimony of your own con-
" ſcience; and your talents within thoſe
" limits of exertion, in which an undiſcern-
" ing ſpirit has too long ſuffered them to be
" confined. The bird of day however al-
" ways looks to the ſun."—By diſſenting conjectures, does he mean conjectures of the Diſſenters? I ſuppoſe not; though from the contempt he expreſſes, I might think he did. If he means conjectures differing from each other, he ſhould have ſaid diſcordant conjectures:

* Cic. Somn. Scip. Sect. 7.

tures: To diſſent, means to differ from any ſingle opinion as a ſtandard to others. Why did he write Ardelios with a capital letter? and why did he not tranſlate it into buſy bodies, among his other tranſlations? for it is as little intelligible to thoſe who do not underſtand Latin, as any other Latin word; and it is not every body that has read Martial, or remembers Phædrus: But, if he never thinks of theſe curious people, why talk of them, if his vanity is not a little gratified by exciting curioſity? and even his friend he is deſirous ſhould be talked of; for to keep a thing a ſecret is rather an odd way to prevent conjectures: But why not let the gentleman diſplay his own talents, if he likes it? and if he does not, why not let him alone? By the bird of day, I ſuppoſe he means the owl, or bird of night, like *lucus a non lucendo;* for there is no other bird that reſembles our Author and his companion in darkneſs. If he wiſhes completely to puniſh him for not publiſhing his works, he need only uſe the revenge of Auſonius, and tell him,

Qui ſua non edit carmina, noſtra legat.——Epig. 34.

If he will not publiſh his own works, let him read mine.

In the quotation from Cicero, he has ſub-

 ſtituted

ſtituted the word *me* for *te*—a ſlight difference, and not forbidden by the laws of quotation, when it is intended to illuſtrate, not to prove, but proper to be remarked, that it may be ſeen where he has quoted an Author literally, and where he has only adapted him.—I muſt frequently have occaſion to object to the Author's mode of punctuation; he for ever begins a ſentence with a conjunction or an adverb,—an *if*, or an *and*.

" And when I have commanded a ſilence " within my own breaſt, I think a ſtill ſmall " voice may whiſper thoſe gratulations, from " which an honeſt man may beſt derive com- " fort from the paſt, and motives for the fu- " ture action." The ſilence is not within his own breaſt, for there the matter is known, but to the world. The words ' ſtill ſmall voice' are not marked as a quotation, though they are taken from 1 *Kings* xix. ver. 12.

Before he claims the character of an honeſt man, let him reflect whether any thing can be honeſt which ſhuns the light; and as to his comfort, I do not envy him,—the comfort of having made miſchief and quarrels.

" The wayward nature of the time, and " the paramount neceſſity of ſecuring to this

" king-

" kingdom her political and religious exiſt-
" ence, and the rights of ſociety, have urged
" and ſtimulated me, as you well know, to
" offer *this endeavour* to preſerve them, by a
" ſolemn, laborious, and diſintereſted appeal
" to my countrymen."—The political exiſtence of a nation, ſignifies her exiſtence as a political eſtabliſhment of men living together in civil ſociety, but they may exiſt as a nation without a religious eſtabliſhment; therefore the expreſſion is faulty, it is inappropriate; the rights of Society do not depend upon any form of government: The Poles are the only people who have loſt their political exiſtence as a nation during the preſent conteſt. That his appeal is ſolemn, no one will deny; that it is laborious, appears from his manner of writing; but that it is diſintereſted, we have no evidence.

" *Vitæ est avidus, quiſquis non vult, mundo*
" *ſecum pereunte, mori.*"—This is one of the quotations to which our Author has left me to ſupply the reference; it is taken from the chorus to the fourth act of the tragedy of Thyeſtes.

" Yet I ſee, with ſorrow and fear, the po-
" litical conſtitutions of Europe falling a-

" round

" round us, or crumbling into duſt, under the " tyrannical Republic of France."—In moſt quarrels which laſt a long time, the original ground of diſpute is apt to be forgotten; ſo it is in the preſent conteſt: The French have forgot that they were urged to the war in defence of their liberty; and the Coalition on the Continent has forgot that they undertook it for the defence of Deſpotiſm.—Let the Author remember this, and he will ſee why the political conſtitutions of Europe are crumbling to duſt, day by day.

" She has indeed terminated in the change " or overthrow of each of them, *but of this* " *kingdom.*"—Does our Author mean to ſay, that we have experienced no change ſince the commencement of the war? he will doubtleſs ſay it is for the better, and I ſhould be ſorry to differ from him on ſo *nice* a point. ' Each' is an improper word, it ſhould be *all; each* means *either of two* in proſe.

" Frenchmen were always brutal, when " unreſtrained." So will all nations, who have been long reſtrained; for the natural ſucceſſor of Deſpotiſm is Anarchy. Let me here aſk the Author, whether it is more conſonant to the ſpirit of Chriſtianity to lament and en-

deavour

deavour to ſoften ; or to exult in, and enflame national antipathies ? Philoſophy weeps over, and wiſhes to alleviate the miſeries of mankind ; and is Chriſtianity leſs mild, leſs gentle and benevolent ?

Our Author's ſtile is a tiſſue of quotations in the next ſentence. The whole of this metaphor is borrowed from *Jeremiah* v. 8. and is highly poetical both in language and idea ; for the prophets, we all have heard, were poets.

" And when their cruelty is at laſt " wearied out and exhauſted, and demands " a pauſe, they call it clemency." Here we have ' and' beginning a ſentence again, which is contrary to the uſe and propriety of our language. The ſentiment here is borrowed from Tacitus's Life of Agricola, ſect. 30.— *Ubi ſolitudinem fecerunt pacem appellant.*

" France had been long looking for that " which *her philoſophers* had taught her to " term, the PARALLELISM OF THE SWORD; " and ſhe has found it. That ſword has in- " deed ſwept down not only every royal " creſt, but every head which raiſed itſelf " above the plain of their equality."——In which of the French philoſophers our Author has found the ' parallelism of the ſword'

recom-

recommended, I will thank him to point out to me; I have not yet read him. As to their equality, I am afraid he does not comprehend it: It is not equality of riches or of poverty,—but equality of rights, ſecured by equality of repreſentation; and while that principle is preſerved as the fundamental article of their written conſtitution, and called into action once in every year, Frenchmen cannot long be ſlaves, but by their own conſent; and though they have given their executive government great ſtrength to cruſh internal factions and conduct external war, yet the people have not ſurrendered their power for ever; it is ſtill within their reach, and after a peace will be ſoon reclaimed.—Their affairs are now in a critical ſtate, but I will apply to their famous Republic theſe words, from *Racine's Mithridate.*

Plus il eſt malheureux, plus il eſt redoutable.
Act i. Scene 5.

'My ſentence is for open war.'. So ſpake the bloody Moloch; for the illuſtration of whoſe character, I refer my readers to the note on Milton's Paradiſe Loſt, Book ii. l. 43. to try if they can find any reſemblance to that of our Author, when he ſpeaks of war.—What-

Whatever may be his opinion, there are others who think we ſhould have been ſafer if the experiment of Peace had been tried, allowing both ſides to have been doubtful: in my opinion no man is a Chriſtian who will not ſacrifice every thing to peace; ſuch is the literal acceptation of Chriſtianity.

" Among the bands and aſſociated ener-
" gies of England I alſo, in my degree and
" very limited capacity, will ſtruggle for the
" principle of her life."——This affected phraſeology is derived from a Newſpaper called *The World*, which ſome years ago infected our language with new and awkward combinations of words; but this is not our Author's only model, he has looked up to Junius,—but greatly has he failed.

" I feel, in common with the wiſe and re-
" flecting, that the conſtitution of Great-
" Britain, even with its real or apparent
" defects, is worthy of continuance, and I
" hope of perpetuity." To confeſs that our conſtitution has real defects is honeſt; but to wiſh to perpetuate them is more than fooliſh, it is wicked.

" Our anceſtors in 1688 once adopted the
" words of the aged Patriarch, ' We have

" blessed it, yea, and it shall be blessed.' In " this one response, I trust we shall all be " orthodox; and with one heart and voice " condemn all the heresies of Gallic policy, " in the words of the Alexandrian liturgy of " old,—Των αἱρεσιων καταλυσον τα φρυαγματα."

The quotation is from *Genesis* xxvii. 33. but the blessing is worn out: whether we are orthodox in our blessings or our curses, is of little consequence; but it is well when we disguise the vulgarity of the latter in Alexandrian or any other Greek; it shews some idea of shame.

" Government and Literature are now " more than ever intimately connected."— Should our author mean to say that every government ought to feel the force of literature, I will agree with him; but if he means that literature ought to feel the force of Government, there we totally differ. I might enlarge on this subject, if I felt at liberty to express my sentiments; but the times of discussion are past, we must now all think alike.

" I thought it just and right to set before " them excellence opposed to excellence, *

* " Αγαθους αγαθοις αντεξεταζειν. Dion. Halicarn. ad Cne. " Pompeum de Platone Epist. p. 757. Sect. 1. Vol 6. " Ed. Reiske. 1777.

" as well as error contraſted to error. In the " preſent change of manners, opinions, go- " vernment, and learning, you may remem- " ber I gave it as my opinion, in which, after " ſome reflection, you concurred, that a va- " riation is now required in the mode of " conducting ſatirical writing. I mean, by " calling in the reciprocal aſſiſtance of poetry " and proſe in the ſame work, for the great " end; if it is deſigned for general peruſal, " and an extended application. I think this " work is the firſt attempt of the kind, in the " ſenſe which I propoſe."—Does he mean to compare the dull malignity of his own work, with the lively, piercing, candid criticiſm of *Dionysius?* does he mean to ſay that he has followed his good-natured example in ſhewing the beauties of authors before their defects? every page of his book deſtroys the pretence: I will ſhew many inſtances where he has ſpoken only of the *faults* of a writer, without ſaying a word of his *merits* or his *beauties.* There is in this ſentence the ſame want of connection with the reſt, which is to be found in every page of his work. In the quotation, Αγαθες αγαθοις αντεξεταζειν, there is the ſlight variation of αντεξεταζειν for αντεξεταζων. *Contrasted to*, is not Engliſh; it ſhould be, *contrasted with*, good Mr Critic. For what cauſe is it that our Author muſt now vary the mode of ſatirical writing, which has been in uſe, with few exceptions, from the time of Ennius to the preſent day? Was the ſatire of Juvenal and Perſius not ſufficient for the correction of Roman vices? or, are ours greater? I truſt not; the true cauſe of the change is evident: our Author had not room nor power enough in verſe to indulge his private malignity in the detail of anecdote and ſlander: but in truth this is not entirely a new mode of ſatire; the union of *poetry* and *proſe* is as old as the times of *Varro*, and revived by the authors of the *Satire Menippee*, a coarſe invective againſt the framers and adherents of the league formed in 1593, by the Guiſes, againſt the Proteſtant party in France. To him this may be the only literary ſupport left; but I truſt we have yet men of ſufficient genius to defend the cauſe of Virtue and Morality, without tranſgreſſing the bounds of legitimate ſatire. But mark;—he wiſhes his ſatire to be extenſively underſtood, and then come two Greek lines for general peruſal; *for the great end*

end, is an odd expreſſion, and ſnaps off the ſentence rather awkwardly. The Miniſters laugh at our Author's fortifications, which are but mole-heaps compared with the ramparts they have raiſed.*

" I am ſure it cannot be conſtrued into an " *hired ſervice*." If he is, it is more than any body elſe can be: he is perpetually vaunting his own independence, his own conſequence, and his own talents: it was not thus that Junius amuſed his readers; he was wiſer: he knew that no anonymous writer can have credit for more than is evident, which are his talents; therefore he left all the reſt unſaid, but of thoſe he had ſome right to boaſt.

" It is as true in our time, as in that of " Dryden, (I will give you his own words) " that ' the common libellers of the day, are " as free from the imputation of wit, as of " morality.' Satire has another tone and an- " other character." This quotation from *Dryden's Dedication of his Tranſlations of Juvenal and Perſius*, p. 164. ed. 1760. 4th vol. octavo, is

* This ſimile ſeems to ſuit our author exactly: he works under ground like the mole, and has thrown up a few heaps of dirt, which are too trifling either for annoyance or defence.

is rather awkwardly introduced, becaufe only the word *libellers* anfwers his purpofe: he means merely to fay, that fatire is no libel; but the quotation fays much more, which he could not leave out. In the language of an *Apoftle* he fpeaks of the office of a *Satirift*,— '*Magnificabo apostolatum meum.*' Rom. xi. 13. Is not the ftile rather too high?

" Learning is oftentation, cenfure is ma-" lignity." The conftant and ill-judged obtrufion of learning *is* oftentation; and cenfure does proceed from malignity, when it is not impartially beftowed.

" The authorifed inftruments of lawful " war are lawful." This is what the logicians call arguing in a circle: the war is lawful, becaufe the weapons are lawful, and the converfe, without proving either to be fo. Throughout the whole of this paffage, which is too long to infert, he is apprifed of the objection that all fatire is contrary to the letter and the fpirit of Chriftianity; and he has not attempted to anfwer it, but artfully taken another pofition, and attempted to juftify it from the authority of the community. To the bleffing which is pronounced on the meek, he can lay no claim, nor to that on the

merciful

merciful, nor on the peace-makers, for neither meeknefs, mercy, nor peace, are among his good qualities: but he is determined to be the means of enfuring a bleffing to others whom he has reviled, and perfecuted, and fpoke all manner of evil againft, falfely, for Chrift's fake; which are all who differ from his own faith; we have heard the judgment pronounced on him who calleth his brother a fool, and we have heard how many he has called both fools and rogues; we are commanded to love our enemies; but he does not even love his friends.* Judge not, that ye be not judged, Matt. vii. 1. cuts up all his fatire by the roots.—' Thou hypocrite, firft caft the beam out of thine own eye;' but I will purfue thefe charges no further; they are fufficient to condemn him with any one who takes the gofpel literally; and who has authorifed us to give it another meaning? Jefus Chrift followed literally what he preached to others.

" Satire never can have effect, without a " perfonal application." I agree with him that fatire lofes its effect when not addreffed to

* Matt. v. 44. & Note (*b*) Dial. 2d.

to individuals, for what is general no man will apply to his own character, if it is againſt him; but an author who names others, is bound by the laws of honour and honeſty to give his own name: if he advances what is falſe, the law will puniſh him; if what he knows to be true, he ſhould be allowed to prove it: then all is fair both parties.

" It never has its full force, if the author " of it is known or ſtands forth; for the " unworthineſs of any man leſſens the " ſtrength of his objections. This is a full " anſwer to thoſe who require the name of " a ſatirical poet."——If this is true, the ſatiriſts of former times have done little good, and our author muſt be the moſt efficacious that has ever written; but even his dogmatical ſtile will not convince the public that they have not a right to know the name of every author; and it is far from a full ſatisfaction to thoſe who ſuffer an injury, to be told it is for the public good that they ſhould not know from whom it comes; to be both criminal and judge is rather too much at once.

" But I may aſk with confidence,—Is " there, in this work on the Purſuits of Li-

" terature

" terature, any ſentence or any ſentiment, by " which the mind may be depraved, degra- " ded, or corrupted? Is there a principle of " claſſical criticiſm in any part of it, which is " not juſt and defenſible by the greateſt maſ- " ters of ancient and legitimate compoſi- " tion?" I anſwer, that the whole tendency of his book is to deprave, degrade, and corrupt: to inculcate that men and ſtates are no longer ſubject to improvement, that moral and political information are at a ſtand,—is to prepare them for ages of darkneſs and error. Human nature cannot ſtand ſtill:—*Non progredi, et regredi.* The faults of his criticiſms I will afterwards point out.

" Is there any paſſage which pandars to " the vitiated taſte, or to the polluted affec- " tions and paſſions of bad men?" For his purity and his puerility, I recommend him to the readers of *Martial's Coſconius*:

At tua, Coſconi, venerandaque ſanctaque verba,
A pueris debent, virginibuſque legi. Lib. iii. ch. 69.

" Is there any idle, depreciating declama- " tion againſt the real and ſolid advantages " of birth, fortune, learning, wit, talents, and " high ſtation?" But he has neglected to

D ſhew

ſhew what are the real and ſolid advantages of birth and fortune.

" If they are inclined to *indict* any part of " my work as *libellous*, it will be incumbent " on them to contradict the great ſage of " the law, * who declares, that *In a* CRIMI- " NAL PROSECUTION, *the tendency which all* " *libels have to create animoſities and diſturb the* " *publick peace*, IS THE WHOLE *which the law* " *conſiders*." Since he has appealed to Blackſtone, by Blackſtone he muſt be tried; and Blackſtone will condemn him. Can any thing tend more to create animoſities and diſturb the public peace, than anonymous ſatire extenſively applied, and extenſively diffuſed? Does not he, who feels that he is injured in his character or fame by an enemy in ſecret, look with ſuſpicion and diſtruſt on every man he meets? Is not the confidence of familiar intercourſe mortally wounded, when no man of any celebrity can feel at eaſe in any company, leſt the man that ſits next him ſhould be the man that has defamed him? The ſatiriſts of old were known and avoided by the vicious and the fooliſh, who could cry out when they ſaw them, *fœnum*

* Blackſtone's Comment. book 4. ch. 11.

*fænum habet in cornu;** but now even the virtuous are not ſafe from the danger of being miſrepreſented. Let the Author boaſt of his zeal and public ſpirit, his love of the conſtitution, his purity and benevolence, yet I will venture to affirm, that no Jacobin that ever wrote, has done more to injure private happineſs and diſturb the peace of ſociety, than this zealous advocate of virtue and morality.—When he ſpeaks of public books, he ſhould not include the Priapus, which was never publiſhed.

" In this work, I have not violated the " precepts of Chriſtianity, or the law of the " land; and till I have done both, or either, " it is not in the power of any man to de- " grade my character and reputation with " my country." That he has not violated the precepts of Chriſtianity is falſe; for its great precept 'do unto others as you wiſh them to do unto you' is violated by anonymous ſlander; but as its language is not always ſo gentle, our Saviour's reproofs of the Phariſees are the model he has choſen for the ſtile of his cenſure: with reſpect to the law of

* Horat. Sat. 1. lib. 4. l. 34.

of the land, it is not known how far a man may go without being deemed libellous.

" If I have drawn any ſuppoſed charac-" ters, without a name or deſignation, I have " done no more than Theophraſtus or La " Bruyere." He has done much more than theſe writers, for he has mentioned many individuals by name, and drawn characters of others whom he durſt not name, which no one can poſſibly miſtake. *

" The '*ſume ſuperbiam*' † of a poet is " ſeldom ſeverely examined. It is an ex-" travaganza at moſt, and underſtood as " ſuch." But the '*ſume ſuperbiam*' of an anonymous writer is truly ridiculous; it is an extravaganza, and laughed at as ſuch.

" I may add, that it would be difficult to " analyze one of the moſt finiſhed ſatires in " our language, I mean Pope's Two Dialo-" gues, or, as they are ſtrangely called, The " Epilogue to the Satires." I do not ſee why they are called the Epilogue, more ſtrangely, than the other dialogue is called the Prologue to the Satires; for prologue and

* *Vide* Note (*o*) to Dialogue 2d. and the Character of Dr Moroſophos.

† Horat. Od. lib. iii. p. 30. v. 14.

and epilogue are no more than introduction and conclusion of any performance.

" I am represented as having threatened " any person who makes enquiry after me " or my name." He has threatened: when he says, to those who enquire after his name, ' there is a darkness which may be felt,' what is that but to say, he will make them suffer for their temerity.

" I maintain it boldly; no man has a right " to demand either my name or my situa- " tion." For an anonymous writer to talk of his boldness, is rather ludicrous; but notwithstanding this, I maintain it with more than equal boldness, that every man has a right to know by whom he is injured or insulted.

" For I believe I have no real enemies, but " the lovers of confusion and the troublers " of states." Our Author has a strange way of beginning a sentence with an adverb, and it is not easy here to see the force of this inference, or its truth, as a simple proposition; for, I believe, it is in my power to tell him of many whom he has made his enemies, who never have lain under the imputation of being *troublers* of *states*, or *adversaries to any establishment*.

" If

" If I am forced indeed to deſcend into the " lower regions of ſorrow and confuſion, " among the perturbed ſpirits of anarchy " and democracy, I ſhall hope for the ſafe " conduct of the Sibyll. She might produce " the branch to the ferryman of France and " Tartarus. I would wiſh her to exhibit " this Pöem, as the ' Donum fatalis virgæ, " longo poſt tempore viſum." Into what ſtrange confuſion does his itch for quotation lead him: firſt he is *Diomede* before the walls of Troy, then he is *Eneas* deſcending to Hell: but in this laſt character, I doubt, his branch will be of little uſe to him, for it is not a branch of olive.

" My book is open to all the accumulated " ſeverity of public criticiſm, and public re- " prehenſion. I ſhrink from neither of them. " When I am wrong, (I have never been ſo " intentionally) I will correct myſelf, and I " have done ſo frequently. In a field ſo ex- " tenſive, candour, I think, will allow that " my miſtakes have not been very numer- " ous." It is not his miſtakes that will bring upon him the accumulated ſeverity of public criticiſm, but his intentional faults, the egotiſm and arrogance of his manner, the affect-

ed

ed pompofity of his ftile, the bigotry of his principles. *Verfification*, does not fignify *verfe*, as our Author has ufed it, but the *ftructure* of *verfe*; at leaft I apprehend fo.

" I offer the poetry to thofe who are con-" verfant with the ftrength, fimplicity, and " dignity of Dryden and Pope, and them " alone. I fubmit both my Poems, ' The " Purfuits of Literature, and The Imperial " Epiftle,' in this fpirit and with this confi-" dence to the public. There are men (and " women too) who underftand. But as to " the lovers of exotic poetry, I refer them " to the Botanic Garden of Dr Darwin. My " plants and flowers are produced and che-" rifhed by the natural invigorating influ-" ence of the common fun; I have not raif-" ed them by artificial heat." To fpeak of thefe qualities, belonging equally to Pope and Dryden, fhews a want of judgment not to be tolerated in a man who fets up for a guide of the public Tafte. Dryden certainly has them all, and Pope has ftrength and dignity; but Dryden's is the ftrength of a Doric, Pope's of a Corinthian pillar; he is elegant, delicate, and refined; he is any thing but fimple. The character of fimplicity belongs moſt to Parnell of any poet in our language, and among the ancients to Theocritus. Has Pope any reſemblance to theſe writers? I think not. If our Author does, I am ſorry to differ from him: but I differ from him yet more, if he thinks he poſſeſſes any of the qualities as a poet, he has juſt enumerated; and it is ſomewhat ſingular, that all the faults which he has attributed to Dr Darwin's poetry, are to be found in his own proſe, which is a garden of exotics from all countries.

"I would ſhew, that I am ſtrictly impar-" "tial." Does he underſtand what the word impartial means?

"It is to miſunderſtand or to miſrepreſent" "me, when it is aſſerted that I attack alike" "friends and foes. I attack no man in his" "*individual* capacity." This is falſe; for he has attacked many men for things which relate to them only as individuals, witneſs Pepper Arden's perſon, and Dr Lawrence's poverty. He has never been accuſed of being too ſevere on his friends; his great error is, that he is too blind to their faults.

"I will never give a proof of my ſpirit at" "the expence of my underſtanding." Let him

him rather ſay at the expence of his perſon; for I believe there are a good many cudgels ready for him.

" I would not have you, or any man, " think, that I enter into a defence of my " work, as if I thought it required one."— Matchleſs arrogance! The egotiſm and vanity of this man are beyond all bearing: it was not thus that the great ſatiriſts of former times ſpoke of themſelves. I have counted in one page, (p. 16.) the word *I* no leſs than ſeventeen times repeated, and *my* five times, which is more by two-thirds than can be found in any other writer, and twenty-two times more than any Mr *Nobody* has a right to uſe.

" My countenance is unaltered." So is that of any man who wears a maſk: the pompous egotiſm of this page is wound up by a quotation from Livy, which, in the general ſtile of his quotations, is made out with many words of his own; as he has choſen to give only a part, I will give the reſt, and the readers may judge which beſt applies to him: the hiſtorian ſpeaks of Appius Claudius, a conſtant enemy and hater of the people:— ' *Tribunos et plebem et ſuum judicium pro nihilo*

 habebat:

habebat : illum non minæ plebis, non ſenatus preces perpellere unquam potuere, non modo ut veſtem mutaret, aut ſupplex prenſaret homines ; ſed ne ut ex conſueta quidem aſperitate orationis (quum ad populum agenda cauſa eſſet) aliquid leniret atque ſubmitteret: idem habitus oris, eadem contumacia in vultu, idem in oratione ſpiritus erat: adeo ut magna pars plebis Appium non minus reum timeret, quam conſulem timuerat. Semel cauſam dixit quo ſemper agere omnia ſolitus erat accuſatorio ſpiritu.'—Lib. ii. Sat. 61. With reſpect to the propriety of quotation, I mean to ſpeak hereafter; as to the rules of it, as eſtabliſhed by the uſe of the beſt writers, I will ſay a few words now: hiſtorical and philoſophical quotation ſhould be literal, exact, and complete, both as to the words and the ſpirit of the author, or it may be uſed to bad purpoſes : to illuſtrative quotation, a greater latitude is allowed; words may be uſed with a different application from what they had originally, and the whole of a paſſage need not be produced, provided the ſpirit of the Author is retained, but then the quoter is ſubject to have the remainder turned againſt him : humorous quotation admits of ſtill greater liberty; a writer is permitted to do any thing but change the words, or or put in others; but this our Author has not hesitated to do even in serious quotations, which totally destroys his credibility from henceforth. Another thing required in all quotations, is to be exact in the references.

" I hate deserters of their duty, * on any " principle whatever." And so do I: for once we agree. Though the cause of the seceders has been pleaded with as much argument as it will admit by that incorruptible patriot, the Rev. Christopher Wyvill, it is not to be defended; the question is a plain one, and reducible to a few words; let those men resign their seats whom circumstances prevent from doing their duty; if they will not, let them persevere as the apostle says, ' by honor and dishonor, by evil report and good report, as deceivers and yet true,'† ' let them fight the good fight, let them be stedfast even to the end:'‡ it is by perseverance only that the best cause can be gained, and sometimes even the worst. They occupy the place of others whom their constituents might choose; and they neglect the only means that is left, during the silence of the press, of speaking to the people.

" But

* H. of C. Nov. 1797.

† 2 Cor. vi. 8. ‡ 2 Tim. iv. 7.

" But I ſuppoſe ſome Stateſmen think, that " there is a laudable obliquity and a ſeaſon- " able fear. For my own part I ſhall not on " this occaſion, invade the retreat of St Ann's " Hill, or violate the purity of Drury-Lane. " If *ſuch* Stateſmen are reſolved to free at " once both the Senate and the Throne, the " ' Sævi Spiracula Ditis' are open to them; " they may deſcend in ſafety, and diſburthen " the land." This paſſage is in the true ſtile of its Author: it is in ſome parts unintelligible, in others brutal, and in all conceited. That any man ſhould think obliquity of conduct to be laudable, is impoſſible; it may appear uſeful, but never right: his affected delicacy towards the retreat of St Ann's Hill, only ſerves to diſplay the deep malignity of his ſentiments, againſt the moſt enlightened ſtateſman the world can at preſent boaſt; and his alluſion to Drury-Lane is a far-fetched ſneer at the proprietor of that theatre: but when he tells us that ſuch ſtateſmen may go to the devil, if they pleaſe, he ſhews, in full light, the bitter rancour of his ſpirit, that could rejoice to deprive the world of the moſt ſplendid talents, merely becauſe they are exerted in a cauſe to which he is oppoſed.

oppoſed. If he ſpeaks only in metaphor, it is fooliſh; if he is ſerious, it is wicked; but if the land muſt be diſburthened, let it be of thoſe by whom it has been burthened.

" On the broad general queſtion of the " time, the public eſteem has been commen- " ſurate with the royal approbation." A happy imitation of the affected phraſeology of the *World;* and a ſtrong violation of that plainneſs and ſimplicity of ſtile which the beſt writers have exemplified, and the beſt critics have enforced.

" The noble Marquis, who is no more in " office, may brood ſafely over beads and " relicks." The malignity of the Author's temper is perhaps never more evident than in this cold ſneer at the Marquis of Buckingham, for his protection of a ſet of wretched emigrant prieſts: the reſt of the paſſage requires an interpreter.

" I was not formed to wait in the anti- " chamber of a Duke of Lerma, or a Don " Calderone." It is not my intention to become a commentator to our Author's works, or to explain his obſcure alluſions; but ſometimes, when it ſuits my purpoſe, I will purſue what he has begun, when it does not go to any

great

great length ; to many of my readers it will ſave much trouble, to be told that the Duke of Lerma was the imperious miniſter of Philip the Third of Spain, that Don Rodirigo Calderona was the miniſter's favourite ; and that, after enjoying and miſuſing the utmoſt plentitude of power, they both experienced an ignominious and deſerved death. The character of the latter is thus drawn by a living author, who finiſhed *Watſon's* Life of Philip III. ' His temper, naturally violent and impetu-' ous, was unreſtrained by any of thoſe conde-' ſcenſions and regards which are ſo neceſſary ' in his ſituation, to ſoothe jealouſy and diſ-' arm the rancour of envy ; he mingled in ' all the intrigues of the court, *he delighted* ' *in the exerciſe of power, his favour was the* ' *ſureſt road to preferment, and this he diſtributed,* ' *for the most part, according to his own fancy and* ' *caprice, and without any regard to merit or pre-*' *tenſions ;* he had audiences as if he had been ' a ſovereign prince, held frequent conſulta-' tions, and ſhared, in one word, the admini-' ſtration of public affairs with the Duke of ' Lerma. The haughtineſs and impetuoſity ' of Don Rodirigo was contraſted, by the ' decent moderation which appeared in the

' whole

'whole conduct and deportment of his fa- 'ther." Vol. ii. 156. I will only add, that two years of imprisonment softened his temper, and that his patience under his afflictions cast a lustre on his latter end, which never brightened his prosperity. Our author, I suppose, has never heard of him but in Gil Blas, for he spells his name with an *e* at the end; historians, who understand Spanish, with an *a*.

"But if the laurel, which I have *now* "planted, should thicken round the temple "of my retirement, the pillars will support "it. The materials are solid, and the ground "is firm." For ever writing in metaphors: the materials of his temple are certainly meant to allude to his character and talents; if so, what confusion has he created, with his pillars, and his temples, and his laurels, which in the same passage, are to mean different things?

"I have indeed a few memoirs by me, "written in other days and with other hopes, "and if I could polish the stile, and reduce "them a little into form, I am convinced "they would not be uninteresting. 'Le "Roi et ses Ministres peutetre se fairoient "lire ces Memoires, qui assurement ne sont "pas ceux d'un ignorant.' But let this pass

" for the prefent." This paffage is another proof of his high opinion of his own confequence, and his quotation is another inftance of his talent in that way; it is of his own making, for I neither find nor remember any fuch paffage in Gil Blas, the book he quotes. Thefe memoirs will, perhaps, let us into a fecret; for it will be difficult for him to publifh memoirs, without letting the world know who he is, or leading to fomething that may betray him.

" I am for practicable politicks. I would " not be driven into meafures from which " there is no retreat. I fmile when I am told " of love and hate in politicians and mini- " fters. Thefe are paffions which they never " felt. Circumftances alone unite and fepa- " rate them." A happy fpecimen of ftile; five fhort fentences together: there is at times an oracular brevity in the Author's manner, which he wifhes to have thought conceals fomething, to give him confequence. That the generality of politicians conceal their love and hatred when it fuits their intereft, every man knows; but that they do not feel thefe emotions as well as other men, our Author has for the firft time difcovered: he looks

looks only to the present ministry, and thinks he is drawing a character of human nature, at all times. That they do not love nor hate each other, is true; but that there are no men whom they do not hate, is false. "Suffers the nature of an insurrection." *Julius Cæsar*, act ii. scene 1.

"I look around me. I look to human ac-
"tions, and to human principles. I consider
"again and again, what is the nature and
"effect of learning and of instruction; what
"is the doctrine of evidence, and the foun-
"dation of truth. I ask myself, are all these
"changed? Have the moral and the natural
"laws of God to his creatures another basis?
"Has the lapse of fifty years made an altera-
"tion in HIM, who is declared to be THE
"SAME to-day, yesterday, and for ever?*
"Can the violence, the presumption, the
"audacity, the arrogance, the tyranny of
"man, drunk with self idolatry and tempo-
"rary success, change the nature and essence
"of GOD and of his works, by calling good
"evil and evil good? I am told, that human

* Heb. xiii. 8. By inverting the words, he has destroyed the harmony of the period: the apostle writes '*the same yesterday, to-day, and for ever.*"

" reafon is nearly advanced to full perfec-
" tion; I am affured, that fhe is arrived at
" the haven where fhe would be. I again
" look around me. I afk, where is that ha-
" ven? where is that fteady gale which has
" conducted her? I liften; but it is to the
" tempeft: I caft my view abroad; but the
" ocean is every where perturbed. I paufe
" again. Perhaps, it is *the wind and storm*
" *fulfilling* HIS *word!*" Is this argument? Or is it declamation? Or is it downright folly? If he can ever be brought to think that thefe things are the deeds of Providence, as, in the laft words, he feems to intimate, how can he either complain or be difmayed? The quotation is from the 146th Pfalm, and is 'ftormy wind' not 'wind and ftorm.'

" I refume the reflections of fuffering hu-
" manity amid the wreck of intellect. This
" was not the ancient character of Philofo-
" phy. The lovers of wifdom, in the beft
" ages of Athens and of Rome, always dif-
" courfed with reverence and fubmffiion to
" the Author and Governor of the world." If he means that none of thefe Philofophers indulged themfelves in fcepticifm, I muft tell him, he has yet to read Cicero's Philofophical Works

Works, and the lives of the Philoſophers by Diogenes Laertius. On many ſuch as theſe the light of Revelation did ſhine without enlightening them, according to our Author's wiſh: and it is the boaſt of the apoſtle, 'that God had choſen the weak things of the world to confound the mighty:' 1 *Cor.* i.

" If to their ribaldry they join folly and " groſs ignorance, they ſhould be driven " from our fellowſhip with contempt. The " continued labours of the arch Theoma- " chiſt of the age, the records of that perpe- " tual conflict which he maintained, during " the courſe of fifty years of a long and im- " pious life, againſt the ſpiritual 'kingdoms " of God and of his Chriſt,' and the memo- " rials of his deſolating days, will all be en- " tombed in the French Pantheon with the " mouldering remnant of his bones. 'Duſt " to duſt: aſhes to aſhes.' He ſowed unto " the fleſh, and of the fleſh he and his diſci- " ples have reaped death and corruption." It was not thus that the Saviour of mankind and his great apoſtle ſought to convince the learned among the Jews and the Greeks: they preached to them patiently; they were inſtant in ſeaſon, and out of ſeaſon; they re-

 proved,

proved, rebuked, and exhorted, confident of the truth of their doctrine: * and are the infidels of the present day, coldly to be dismissed with contempt? this argues either too great confidence, or great distrust. Let the Christian philosopher, if he believes his religion to be true, rather imitate the unwearied labours of the arch Theomachist, who for fifty years never remitted his literary warfare against the strength and the weakness of Christianity: time only can decide whether his efforts were directed by a spirit of impiety or sound wisdom: neither our dogmatical Author, nor any individual, is a competent judge of a point which requires the test of ages to determine. Our Saviour was crucified as a blasphemer.

" All the minor powers of infidelity, anar-
" chy, sedition, rebellion, and democracy,
" may *yet* be dispersed *in England;* from their
" leaders Voltaire, D'Alembert, and Condor-
" cet, to the vulgar illiterate blasphemy of
" Thomas Paine, and the contemptible non-
" sense of William Godwin. I feel for man-
" kind when they are insulted by such wri-
" ters. I make common cause with my fel-
low-

* 2 Tim. iv. 2.

" low-creatures, and call upon them to rally " round the conſtitution of our human na- " ture, and to ſupport its dignity." Our Author has not told us how they are to be diſperſed, but he has given us room to gueſs; there is an engine which he admires more than the preſs, that might do great things; he longs to ſet it to work: it is an engine powerful for a time, but not irreſiſtible; it may ſtifle the truth, but never can ſuppreſs it; for truth has an elaſticity that will always rebound, while error can never long prevail unleſs it is ſupported; error therefore need not be ſuppreſſed; truth cannot, tho' perhaps it can never be generally prevalent.— But I will not reſt in looſe generalities; I will define what I mean by truth and error: truth is the nature and relation of things to each other; the knowledge of theſe is philoſophy, which is divided into natural and moral; the means of arriving at this knowledge, is in the firſt inſtance experiment; in the ſecond inſtruction: philoſophy, thus defined, is limited to the things of the natural and moral world: to this, error is the oppoſite. To act according to the moral relations of things is virtue; the contrary is vice, which proceeds

from

from ignorance. Thus have I attempted briefly to define the ſum of human Philoſophy: to this, if it be objected that a ſufficient motive is wanting for action, I will anſwer, that happineſs, which is the object of every man's conduct, is motive ſufficient; and if a ſanction is required, there can be none higher. I will now return to our Author, with his minor and his major powers of democracy, and remark, that with ſingular ingenuity he has included the greater in the leſſer, when he tells us, that the minor powers of infidelity might be diſperſed, from Voltaire down to Godwin and Paine; this is liberal in the deſign, and is ingenious in the execution: it is a pity it is not quite intelligible.

" From writers of this character, my " thoughts are directed to the profeſſors of " *that ſuperſtitious corruption* of Chriſtianity, " which *originally* gave occaſion to thoſe at- " tempts, to which it has pleaſed Providence " to permit a temporary ſucceſs, to ſcourge " the nations of Europe. I am ſure the plain " ſimplicity of the Proteſtant religion of " England could never have ſuggeſted ſo " daring, ſo extenſive a project. I have " there-

" therefore ſpoken at large of the Roman " Catholic religion, *and* its profeſſors, *and* " the emigrants *and* French prieſts."—— From infidelity to popery, is not the common tranſition, rather the reverſe; but I give our Author credit for ſeeing any connection between the two. This is perhaps the moſt extraordinary paſſage in the whole book, for the arrogance, illiberality, and ignorance, it diſplays. Our Author is here hand in glove with Providence: in ſhort, nothing is hid from him; he can tell to an iota the cauſes of all the great events in the world. Popery gave occaſion to the French Revolution; the ſucceſs of that Revolution is only temporary, and meant to puniſh the reſt of Europe who have corrupted Chriſtianity, I ſuppoſe: but the beſt of all this is, that our author knows and is convinced that the Proteſtant religion is plain and ſimple, that there are no difficulties in its creed, no follies in its diſcipline, no contradictions in its liturgy, and that our biſhops can boaſt an uninterrupted ſucceſſion from Chriſt and his apoſtles: ſo thought the papiſts, and ſo think they ſtill; and who is to decide between us? but I had forgot, our Author is the judge, and all is right.

right. Alas! I doubt we have no infallible criterion but time for all the opinions of men; with our Author, their truth or error depends on their being eſtabliſhed or not; and if he had lived in the days of Popery, he muſt have died a Papiſt: ſo much for his judgment. Let the author conſult Longinus and Quinctilian, to be inſtructed how frequent copulatives enervate the ſtile of a writer.

" From ſome obſervations I have heard " and ſeen on this part of my work, you may " remember I was tempted to think, that I " had advanced ſomething new on this ſub- " ject. I am ſure the principles are as old " and as moderate as thoſe of the Reforma- " tion. I know that every page of our hiſ- " tory confirms their truth." I adviſe him not to be too forward in claiming any reſemblance to the reformers, leſt he ſhould be ſuſpected of borrowing ſome of the moderation of John Knox, of Calvin, or Elizabeth. As to the example of hiſtory, it is nothing: for how can the hiſtory of the Reformation be compared to the preſent times: are the papiſts as numerous, as powerful, as ſore from recent injury, as they were then? What he has advanced

vanced on the ſubject of Popery is very old, and therefore does not apply to our times.

" I only declared and pronounced ſolemnly " in the face of my country, that A COL- " LEGE OF ROMISH PRIESTS of a religion " hoſtile in principle and in action too, " whenever it has the power, againſt the " eſtabliſhed church of this kingdom, *ſhould* " *not be ſet upon a hill*, and authoriſed and " maintained by the miniſters of the crown, " and the publick money of the land." Our Author's violence againſt the Romiſh Clergy ſomewhat reſembles in ſpirit, tho' I will do him the juſtice to ſay, not in language, a coarſe invective under the quaint title of Gideon's Cake of Barley Meal; there is the ſame intolerance, the ſame narrowneſs, the ſame virulence in both: but in the heat of his zeal againſt Popery, he has overlooked the real grounds of danger, which is in the tendency our own Clergy have ſhewn to a nearer connection with the Romiſh church: ſince the commencement of the preſent war they have declared what ſpirit they are of; a ſpirit which reſembles that of their papiſt brethren, in aiding the deſigns of the ſtate: in unqualified terms they have preached up

 blood-

bloodſhed and murder; they have forgot that they are miniſters of a church whoſe foundation is peace, the church of Chriſt; and plainly ſhewn that they are ready to be miniſters of any church that will pay them; no matter to them how Chriſtianity is violated, if it ſerve their purpoſes. In addition to this, others of them have ſhewn a ſtrong leaning towards Popery in their doctrines; I allude to a ſermon preached at St Mary's, Oxford, by Henry Beſt, of Magdalen College, 1794; to a pamphlet called Hopes and Expectations, by Faulder, 1793; to a Series of Diſcourſes, by Robert Foley, of Oriel College, 1795, where the ſame infallibility is claimed for the Proteſtant, as for the Popiſh church; to Sermons by Robert Gray, preached at the Bampton Lecture, and to the Eſſay on the church by the Rev. Mr Jones of Neyland; in all theſe a ſtrong tendency to unite with the Catholics on moderate principles, that is to ſay, the Proteſtants invite the Catholics to ſoften ſome of their moſt obnoxious doctrines, and they are willing to concede a few inſignificant points, for the ſake of adopting the arbitrary principles of the Catholics both in church and ſtate; but if this invitation is refuſed, fufed, they have demonftrated that they have a religion of their own that will equally anfwer their purpofe. See Monthly Review for 1797, part 1ft, p. 81. Their object is to deftroy the right of private judgment on which our Proteftant church was erected, and to prevent the propagation of religious enquiry by the means of an infallible church. If there is any ground of alarm, it is here, and our Author, in the excefs of his zeal, has not, to ufe a vulgar faying, put the faddle on the right horfe; he has neglected to accufe our own clergy of making the firft advances, who are therefore the moft dangerous, and deferve moft to be blamed. For fome ftrong facts on this fubject, I refer my readers to a letter to the Marquis of Buckingham, Owen, 1796; and laftly, for a proof of this popifh fpirit among our clergy, I refer to Daubigny's Guide to the Church, lately publifhed. Here I leave our Author for the prefent on this popifh fubject, to dream of racks, torture, and inquifitions: fhould Popery be re-eftablifhed in his life time, he ftands a chance to be the firft martyr to the *odium theologicum* of popifh priefts, which he has taken fuch pains to excite; but I will

 ceafe

ceaſe to terrify him, for between popery and atheiſm, I doubt the poor man is never eaſy day nor night.

"But, 'though I give all my goods (ſaid " an Apoſtle) to feed the poor and the diſ- " treſſed, and have not *Charity*, it profiteth " me nothing.' What does he mean? He " ſurely means ſomething. Alms alone, it " ſeems, however liberal, however extended, " neither are, nor can be, the whole or the " eſſence of Chriſtian charity." Let us here remark how the words of the apoſtle, 1 Cor. xiii. 2, 3, 4, 5, 6, 7, are made to ſuit the deſigns of our Author; he quotes a part of a paſſage, and then twiſts it to his own purpoſe, ſo that the general comprehenſive philanthrophy of the apoſtle is frittered down till it means at laſt nothing but conſtitutional toleration; a meaning unknown to the extenſive benevolence of Chriſtianity: remark, reader, the proceſs, he ſagely obſerves, that when the apoſtle ſpeaks of charity, he means ſomething, and that he cannot means alms as the whole of charity, ſo far I will agree with him; but here we ſeparate, for when he talks of its being a principle of general ſafety, of diſcernment, of prudence, and of guarded

guarded virtue, he ſpeaks of ſomething ſuited to the worldly ſpirit of a politician, but not to a follower of Chriſt, whoſe precept to be wiſe, as ſerpents, was not a general maxim of worldly prudence, but a ſingle admonition to his apoſtles to flee perſecution, till they had fulfilled their miſſion, the converſion of the Jewiſh people.

" Romiſh Baronets will be buſy, and Ro-" miſh Prieſts will meddle. Perhaps the Se-" cretary of that Society knows, whether " theſe hints are true and juſtifiable." If the only Romiſh Baronet who is a member of the antiquarian ſociety is conſcious of deſerving theſe inſinuations, he muſt be a weak man indeed: if he is not, I truſt he will, ſome day or other, have an opportunity of expoſing to contempt, in his proper perſon, the man who throws them out.

" If I am wrong, I fear, I muſt continue " ſo. I have yet ſeen no argument to ſhake " my conviction." This paſſage is a ſuffi-cient clue to moſt of our Author's opinions, moral and political; an invincible obſtinacy and conceit: he never alters an opinion he has once embraced.

" I have been under the neceſſity, at leaſt " as I thought, of appealing for illuſtration

" to writers of all ages and in various lan-" guages." Concerning the propriety of this conſtant appeal to other men's writings, I have frequently had my doubts, and am now more than ever inclined to diſpute it: tho' I do not deny the advantages of a claſſi-cal education, I muſt yet be allowed to repro-bate the frequency of claſſical quotation. The antients, it is true, have left us many models in poetry, hiſtory, oratory, criticiſm, and philoſophy, which will never be ſurpaſſed either in the preſent or future ages, if we are to judge by the progreſs of the world ſince their times; but the uſe we are to derive from them is, to form our taſte and enrich our ideas, not to plaiſter our writings; for he who beſt ſtudies and underſtands, will not be moſt forward to quote them: it ſhews he has read, but not digeſted them; it ſhews that his opinions are not his own; and is a greater evidence of a good memory than a ſtrong judgment: it is moreover, in all works that are intended to be popular, an invincible obſtacle to their being generally underſtood: to tranſlate words, phraſes, or ſentiments, from another language into our own, by which it is improved, is the true end of read-

ing

ing the claſſics; but to tranſplant paſſages, is like patching inſtead of weaving, the one can be done by any bungler who has the materials, the other requires ſome dexterity. No point of mere opinion can be decided by quotation; for the wiſdom of the ancients is on one ſide as well as the other: it is therefore a bad ſubſtitute for argument; for it is eaſy to find a paſſage in ſome author to ſuit any purpoſe. But is quotation never admiſſible? it will be ſaid; undoubtedly it is on many occaſions: in hiſtory it is indiſpenſable, but in works merely of opinion it muſt be uſed ſparingly, and then rather to illuſtrate than to prove. Dryden, Johnſon, and Junius, have ſhewn that genius has little need to be ſupported by quotations, and their writings may ſerve as models how they are to be uſed: our Author, by his prodigality of them, is bringing us back to the antiquated foppery of Jeremy Taylor and his cotemporaries, from which the vigour of Dryden, and the courtly elegance of Sprat had freed us; for they firſt gave the examples of a pure page, and a clear margin; the one had no need of pedantry, the other was afraid of it: ſince their time we have been preſerved from

from this inundation of learned trafh, and the pure ftream of genius has flowed undifturbed by quotation, till Parr and Wakefield, (whofe names I mention with refpect) unwifely poured their exuberant learning thro' their richeft pages: but let me not place thefe men by the fide of our Author for any thing but contraft: their faults fpring from riches, his from extreme poverty; they have no need of the aid of foreign ornament; their ftile and their ideas have only the faults of redundancy; he is for ever on the ftretch to be, what he can never arrive at; and as to quotation, theirs is the murmur of a gentle ftream, compared to his, which refembles the inundation of a torrent.

"No man ever felt the power of poetry, "if he refufed his homage to Dante, Pe-"trarch, Ariofto, and Taffo; I mean, if their "language was familiar to him." To refufe our homage to the Italian poets, and to our Author's pedantry, are two things totally different; tho' he has chofen to put them together.

"In their primal poet there is an origina-"lity and a hardihood of antiquity." For the ufe of the word primal I refer to Johnfon's ſon's Dictionary; he ſays it may be uſed in poetry: and this is one fault of our Author's ſtile; it is too poetical, too metaphorical; his poetry is proſe, and his proſe is poetry.—

> *Eſt enim proxima poetis et quodammodo carmen Solutum, et ſcribitur ad narrandum non ad probandum.*
>
> Quinct. Lib. x. 1.

" Frons læta parum et dejecto lumina " vultu." To this quotation he has given no reference; it is from the 6th Æneid l. 813.

" Ὥσπερ απο των ευωδεστατων λειμωνων αυρα τις ἥδεια " απ' αυτης φερεται. Such is the harmonious proſe " which diſtinguiſhes the critical writings of " the great Halicarnaſſian. Epiſt. ad Cn. " Pompeium. de Platone. Sect. 2." People of nice ears will eaſily diſtinguiſh how the harmony of Dionyſius's proſe is deſtroyed by the repetition of απ' inſtead of ἐξ, in the original,—the ſound and the meaning are equally injured.

" The glory of Spain, Alonzo d'Ercilla." To be the glory of Spain, as a poet, is no very great praiſe: but as I have no knowledge of the Spaniſh language, I will not venture to ſpeak of him, but refer my readers to the French *Dictionnaire Historique*, a work on which it is generally ſafe to rely for its judgment of Authors.

" I am told, I am forgiven for my Latin ; " but for the Greek, not fo eafily. In this " particular indeed, I am rather furprifed " that no man of *wit* has faid of my notes, " *They are Greek invocations to call fools into a* " *circle.* Certainly there will be Halos round " the brighteft luminaries ; and it muft be " confeffed, that many of my notes have " fuch a circular appearance." Had our Author finifhed with his quotation from Shakefpeare, he might have faved his credit ; but to fhew his learning, which I will prove is not very deep, he has written nearly a whole page, which is hardly intelligible : if by the ' brighteft luminaries' he means his own writings, I fear his vanity has outrun his judgment ; but what he means by his notes having a circular appearance, I hope he will explain in his next edition of the tranflations : what any theologian has to do with the validity of his ordination, or what connection there is between ordination and Greek learning, I leave to the clergy to explain ; but I believe the only Greek required for that, is the Greek Teftament.— Next comes a fine flourifh about the Council of Florence, which fome theologians have never

never heard of: if my reader wiſhes for ſome very pleaſant information reſpecting this Council of Florence, they will find it in Mr Gibbon's laſt volume, and ſome more particulars, which he has not related, in Hody's Account of the illuſtrious Greeks; in the Lives of Beſſarion and Chryſoloras; but our Author's information is from Mr *Marſh's* tranſlation of Michaelis, v. 2. whoſe words he has partly copied and partly confuſed, p. 168. He ſays, 'It is ſaid by many of the learned, that at the Council of Florence held in 1439, with a view of eſtabliſhing an union between the Greek and Latin churches, a reſolution was formed that the Greeks ſhould alter their manuſcripts after the Latin.' This is plain and intelligible; but hear our Author, 'the Council of Florence in 1439, when the Greek and Latin churches propoſed that the Greeks ſhould alter their manuſcripts from the Latin.' It is rather ſingular that what was ſo ignominious to the one party, ſhould be propoſed by both; in a diſpute of this kind, where there was no third party to decide, both may agree; but it is not very likely that both ſhould propoſe: but as the gentleman has introduced the ſubject, I will

 purſue

purſue it, and tell him, and thoſe who do not know it, that no ſuch propoſal was ever either made or agreed to ; and if he had read Michaelis a little farther, he muſt have found that it was his opinion, that the whole ſtory aroſe from a diſingenuous fiction of Eraſmus, to cover a defect of his own edition of the Greek Teſtament, in which many paſſages were altered from the Latin, p. 173 and 444 on the editions of the Greek Teſtament." As an additional proof that this is an invention of Eraſmus, we do not find it mentioned by any writer of the hiſtory of that council. Mr Gibbon, whoſe erudition, penetration, and accuracy, were unequalled, has never noticed the circumſtance ; ſo that it happens that this celebrated *Fœdus cum Græcis*, ſo well known to the critics, ſo far as it related to the alteration of MSS. was not known at all, and turns out to be nothing more than a lie. But our Author goes on with Michaelis, and talks of the *capita argumentorum*, in the preface to Eraſmus's edition of the New Teſtament, as if he had read it: when we examine a little further, it appears he has never ſeen it, for he quotes it very pompouſly, Nov. Teſt. by Eraſmus, in 1595, 5th Edition :—

Now

Now Erafmus died in 1536, and publifhed his laft edition of the Teftament in 1535. Is it not very fingular that his error fhould have paffed unobferved through nine editions? if our Author takes the trouble to look over them, he muft have remarked the inaccuracy, had the circumftance been familiar to him.

" And if I were to adduce from the great " Erafmus, my ' Capita argumentorum con- " tra morofos quos dam et indoctos' I fhould " be reminded by Dr Parr, that I have not " the erudition of Erafmus, or the gentle " manners of the ferene Sepulveda. Mr " Knight would remand me to the Greek " alphabet, (to any one, I hope but his own) " and his modefty would attempt fome " jucundity from the Lufus Priapi. I will " endure them all. I have patience and pity " too.' Should Dr Parr deign to think of him at all, he will, no doubt, tell him that he has not the erudition of Erafmus; and I will tell him that he has the manners of the ferene *Sepulveda*, who was a perfecutor and a bigot, *vide* Dict. Hift. but even this expreffion he has borrowed from Michaelis, who fays, v. ii. p. 170. ' but Erafmus had not the gentle manners

manners of Sepulveda'; let our Author remember that the conjunction *nor*, always follows the adverb *not*. I have no patience with our Author; but I have pity for the public, when I see them imposed on by such pompous ignorance.

"He may perhaps improve in calculation; "but I think it will be some time before his "anti-professional prattle will impose on an-"other boy-committee on a contested elec-"tion." This is a reflection on the House of Commons, more severe than any Jacobin ever uttered: to say that that House is partly composed of *boys*, and that what they decide on the most important points is invalid for want of judgment, is a something more than badinage; it is a libel on the Constitution, which entrusts such powers to striplings; but, in fact, both the law and the constitution are justified by experience in admitting persons of twenty-one years of age to be arrived at maturity; and it is only our Author's spleen at the honourable triumph which Mr Tierney gained by that decision, that can dispute its validity. What he means by *anti-professional*, he must hereafter explain; probably he means *extra*-professional: but, after all his badinage,

let

let any honeſt man conſult the proceedings on that petition, and ſay whether the deciſion was not given on the cleareſt principles of law and juſtice. Should the Author tranſlate συνδίκον κλεανον, undoubted right, I will ſuppoſe he has never ſeen Damm's Lexicon to Pindar, who renders them *apta & conveniens poſſeſſio*, a poſſeſſion, apt or ſuitable.

"I am indeed confident, that when all the "perſonal objects of my praiſe or cenſure "ſhall have paſſed from the ſcene, this work "will be found to contain principles of go- "vernment, polity, religion, morality, edu- "cation, criticiſm, poetry, and literature, "worthy of being tranſmitted to another "age." A fine ſentence of Junius is here mangled, to be adapted to the Author of the Purſuits of Literature. Dedication, page 2.

"I have indeed already ſaid much: but I "think, I have ſomething more to offer to "my country, if the bleſſings of ſtrength "and health ſhould graciouſly be extended "and continued to me." I truſt this mighty ſomething means his memoirs, which he has ſpoken of already.

"The dirty family of ſelfiſhneſs, which by "the law of Providence, defeats its own

" purposes." This is a poetical expression from Pope:

> Love, joy, and hope, fair pleasure's smiling train;
> Hate, fear, and grief, the family of pain.
>
> *Essay on Man, Ep.* 2. *l.* 116.

" No man liveth unto himself," is a quotation from Rom. xiv. 17.

" I speak not of a romantic, impracticable " general good, but of the specifick benefit " which an individual may and can confer " on his fellow-creatures." Who ever spoke of any other? The Author contradicts his own words; for *a general good*, is only a good conferred on our fellow-creatures.

" Well-wishers to their country are, above " all things, desirous of the steady light of " Literature, and of the day-spring from on " high.* Yet whatever they or we may hope, " the horizon may perhaps be now illumi- " nated with its departing beams." Our Author is but a poor comforter at any time, but most of all here, if he means to have it understood, that his own poetry is one of the beams of literature, even in her decline.— Others will compare him to a meteor,—to a

* Luke i. 78.

a vapour which blazes for a moment, promifes light, and leads us into darknefs.

" But let us ftill contemplate the glory " which was caft round other times." The glory that was caft round other times, was far different from the fhade with which he has attempted to obfcure the prefent ; the literature, the tafte, the genius, of which he fears the extinction, were all the produce of the beft times of liberty. Poetry can never take a daring flight, but when fhe is free from every reftraint: hiftory and oratory exift only in the funfhine of freedom.

" Satirical glory." To fhew how our Author has twifted and inverted the language, I will cite a few paffages, and leave my reader to fupply the reft, of which he will have frequent opportunities : where the cuftom of the language is to ufe two fubftantives, the fecond in the genitive cafe, he has chofe to put an adjective, as in the words quoted ; and, on the contrary, where the adjective is ufed, he has taken two fubftantives, as in the Allegory of Satire, which means fomething totally different.

" The character of Lucilius, the inventor " of Satire, was refpected by Scipio and

" Lælius. They were his friends. Poetaſters, " rhetoricians, and even men of high quality " and of conſular rank, were often the ſub- " jects of his cenſure." When he ſpeaks here of Lucilius, he has forgot that he is known to us more by the character others have given of him, than by any thing that is left us of his own; and when he tells us that he attacked men of high quality and conſular rank, he ſhould imitate his example, rather than attack thoſe only who are unprotected; but when he tells us, that Lucilius was the inventor of ſatire, he ſeems to forget that the Greeks, or even the Romans, had any ſatiriſts before him: has he never heard of the Margites of Homer, nor the ſatires of Ennius? but Dryden has examined the point much more learnedly in his Dedication of the Tranſlations of Juvenal and Perſius; I will cite one paſſage from him; thoſe who wiſh for more, muſt refer to the original: ' Quinctilian and Horace muſt be cautiouſly interpreted, when they affirm that ſatire is wholly Roman, and a ſort of verſe which was not touched on by the Grecians. The reconcilement of my opinion to the ſtandard of their judgment, is not, however, very difficult, ſince they ſpake

ſpake of ſatire not as in its firſt elements, but as formed into a ſeparate work, begun by Ennius, purſued by Lucilius, and compleated afterwards by Horace. Biſhop Hurd, in his introduction to the Commentary on the Art of Poetry, though his delicacy will not permit him to contradict Horace, plainly ſhews that he did not conſider Lucilius as the inventor of ſatire, for he acknowledges he cannot be conſidered as ſuch on any other ground than that he firſt reduced ſatire into a regular, conſiſtent poem, having a ſingle and main purpoſe, and having but one meaſure: to ſee how looſely the ancients ſpoke, when they call a man an inventor, we need only refer to a paſſage in Paterculus, Lib. ii. ch. 9. where he calls Pomponius the inventor of the Atellane Plays, which Hurd proves he only firſt repreſented in the common dialect; for they had formerly never been written but in the Oſcan, or provincial language of the country.' *Notes on Art of Poetry*, page 189.

" Horace in the politeſt age, under the
" deſpotiſm of Auguſtus, inſinuated himſelf
" into the graces of the Emperor: yet he was
" peculiarly ſtudious to mark the obnoxious,
" fooliſh, or wicked characters of his age.—

 " He

" He was careful not to be misunderstood. " He noted the name, the profession, and the " rank of those whom he devoted to undy- " ing ridicule, or consigned to the eternity " of fame. Augustus and Mæcenas well " knew the value of such a poet." Horace seldom marked the vicious or the foolish among the great; he had therefore no need, like Juvenal and Persius, to disguise what he meant; he was too familiar with a court, to make courtiers the subject of his satire: let the Author blush when he recollects the Emperor whose favour Horace had obtained by the arts of insinuation and flattery;* he exalts to the rank of a god, the subtle subverter of Roman liberty, the crafty tyrant, who purchased power by the semblance of virtue, the incestuous paramour of his own daughter, the murderer of Cicero, and the patron of Tiberius. Tyrants do well to purchase the praises of men of talents, that they may make a decent figure with posterity. We are here to look for our Author's notions of government: Horace is praised for upholding the government of Augustus; the stability of government is connected with literature and

* Od. lib. 3. & *passim.*

and poetry: this he has told us before; (*vide* page 7.) he now tells us what ſort of government: this is honeſt, if it is not prudent.

"In the time of Nero and Trajan, Juvenal "and Perſius exerted a ſeverity without play-"fulneſs." Juvenal never publiſhed one ſatire in the time of Nero, and for one which he wrote in the reign of Adrian, he was baniſhed at the age of eighty, under pretence of receiving a military command; (*vide* his Life by Suetonius and the notes:) ſo much for theſe writers being either ſpared or neglected; that their works were much circulated, (as we now uſe the word) there is no evidence.

"An interval of ages paſſed, dark and barbarous." Has our Author read many of the writings in thoſe ages which are called barbarous? if he has, he ſeems to have forgotten Chaucer. To the ſix poets whom he enumerates, as enjoying the fulneſs of ſatirical glory, I will add one whom he has perhaps never heard of, a ſatiriſt, who, from the difference of times, is not ſo poliſhed as Boileau or Horace, nor ſo cautious in his ſatire, for they lived under deſpots, he under the glory of monarchy, Henry IV. of France. Regnier has all the ſtrength of Juvenal or Perſius,

Perſius, and ſometimes the delicacy of Horace: he has that quick and penetrating ſpirit which pierces through the diſguiſe of forms and faſhions, and ſhews things as they really are. Boileau and Horace laugh at the exterior of vice and folly; Regnier lays them bare; he ſometimes ſees things on the dark ſide, but he who does ſo, will not often be deceived. Regnier led a diſſolute life: he is therefore ſometimes looſe in his ſentiments, but he has a vigour of thought and a ſtrength of expreſſion not equalled by any writer of ſucceeding times. Boileau borrowed, or rather ſtole from him, plentifully: the whole of his addreſs to the king is taken from Regnier; and when we conſider the two monarchs, we muſt ſoon ſee which is the flatterer: Regnier only ſends his kings to heaven, Boileau brings them thence: Regnier has nearly every requiſite for a ſatiriſt, neat and forcible in his expreſſions, ſtrong and vigorous in his ideas; humorous, gay, and ſevere: he wants nothing but the poliſh of a more refined age, to be the firſt ſatiriſt of whom the world can boaſt, in that ſtile of ſatire in which he has written; I will not ſay it is beſt adapted to the purpoſe of a ſatiriſt; becauſe it generally

nerally remains unappropriated ; it therefore fails to correct individuals, but it is of use to instruct, like all general principles of morality : he was the Lucilius of Roman satire, Boileau the Horace. Regnier's satires are not the whole of his works ; the rest consist of epistles, elegies, and penitential odes ; for he began towards the end of his life to feel the effects of his intemperate indulgences, in that debility and languor which are their constant followers. We lament his follies, and pity him for his want of prudence. He was one of those choice spirits whose pleasantry and lively talents purify the grossness of licentious pleasures, but make them at the same time more seductive ; for there is a species of gaiety and humour which belongs only to intemperance ; it finds no amusement in the quiet regularity of virtue, and exists only in the wild sallies of an unbridled genius. This Regnier eminently possessed, and his own epitaph is perhaps the best specimen of it : he could joke with the most serious events of life, and even death did not find him without an epigram. Boileau was the flatterer of despotism, and the persecutor of rival merit ;

he

he has therefore our Author's highest praise; but, like much of his praise and his satire, it is undeserved: he sits down to write with a loose idea of a character, and fills up the rest from his own invention,—' a poet second to none of his predecessors.' He was inferior to Juvenal and Horace, so far as he literally copies them; and where he is original, he has neither the strength of the one, nor the delicacy of the other. His first satire is an imitation of the third of Juvenal; but the object of the two is different: that of Boileau is merely to ridicule a poor discontented author, who rather deserves pity than contempt: the dignified indignation of Juvenal loses all its effect from the mouth of Damon: his satire is directed against the vices of a great and corrupt city; that of his imitator against a pitiful individual, whose works and character are neither of them worthy of notice. The second satire is neat and delicate; the third the same, but not original, for it is taken from Regnier's 10th; the fourth is without doubt the worst; the fifth is far inferior to the eighth of Juvenal: the one marks out his objects with unerring certainty, the other lets fly his arrows at random:

dom: the one is forcibly concise, the other tediously diffuse; the one shews the boldness of a satirist, the other the timidity of a slanderer—he means somebody, but he dare not speak out. What is the feeble line—'*Je vous connais pour noble a ces illustres marques*,' (l. 47.) compared to the two forcible words of Juvenal, '*Agnosco procerem?*' l. 826. The sixth is a continuation of the first, and they both imitate only a part of the third of Juvenal: he describes the vices as well as the dangers of the city, Boileau only the last; and how weak is he, compared with the force, the fire, the strength, the ardour, and the dignity of Juvenal: the seventh is neat and light: his eighth, which is a satire on man, is by no means equal to Pope in his different essays: his ninth is his master-piece; the irony is delicate, the satire pungent; but the objects are not worthy of the weapons: the tenth is a poor imitation of Juvenal's Satire on Women: the eleventh and twelfth, with some brilliant passages, are dull and heavy: on the whole, he might be a gentleman, a courtier, and an elegant writer; but he was not a satirist, if that means a corrector of morals.

" A philoſopher without being wordy, the " friend of ſenſe and of virtue, a gentleman " in principle, independent in ſpirit, and " fearleſs of enemies, however powerful from " their malignity or formidable from their " rank." Is this all that is required of a philoſopher? the Author, I ſuppoſe, meant to ſay a great deal in a few words, and he has ſaid nothing: that he was the friend of virtue, I will not deny; but that he was the enemy of many virtuous men, will be ſeen by turning to the notes to the Amſterdam edition of his works, and the Literary Hiſtory of the Times. Independent in ſpirit that man could not be, who was the ſervile flatterer of the great: and it was no great merit to be fearleſs of enemies, whom he knew had no power to do him harm; for he was encouraged and protected by a court.

" So removed from conceit and forced " thought." Look at the lines 63 and 64 of his Addreſs to the King, and 75, 87, and 88.

" Even his compliments, though rather " lofty, to Louis the fourteenth, are all con- " ceived in the language of a gentleman and " a man of genius, who feels that he is con- " ferring honour, not receiving it." I refer my my readers to the addreſs before-mentioned, but more particularly to lines 3 and 10. but if he has flattered Louis, he has not been leſs attentive to his own praiſe: he magnifies the taſk of praiſing ſo great a monarch: the inference is extremely eaſy. But he has ſpoken plaineſt in line 58, which ſhews his vanity equal to his meanneſs. Since our Author has choſen to inſtitute a compariſon between him and the greateſt maſters of Satire, I alſo will go on with comparing them with him, and with each other, and vindicate the illuſtrious Romans from the unmerited degradation of being lowered to an equality with their modern imitators. Between him and Juvenal or Perſius, there is little reſemblance, either in their ſubjects or their manner. Horace laughs at the follies of mankind, they chaſtiſe their vices: Horace attacks inſignificant characters, they ſtrike only at the higheſt: Horace never goes beyond a ſneer, they never excite a ſmile: even Pope is more bold than Boileau, though more delicate than Juvenal or Perſius; they wrote with all the ſpirit of Romans in the beſt times of the Republic, though they lived under the terrors of deſpotiſm; Boileau too lived under a tyrant,

 and

and his writings have the air of a courtier; they ſatiriſed bad men, he only bad writers: as a humorous and didactic poet, he has few equals; but as a ſatiriſt and a man of independent ſpirit, I have thought it right to point out our Author's mis-ſtatement of his character. Whoever wiſhes to ſee his fulſome flattery burleſqued, may read our honeſt *Matt. Prior's* Tranſlation of his Ode on the taking of Namur.

" The majeſty of the French monarch, in " that cultivated age, was ſurely as worthy " of homage as the *deity* of the Roman Au- " guſtus." And both equally worthy of contempt.

" I call their language *ancient*, which ex- " iſted before the revolution; for I ſcarce " underſtand the modern democratic jargon. " *Grave virus* munditias *pepulit*." That the French language has received the addition of many new terms ſince the Revolution, is true; new things cauſe new words: but that the literature of France has been corrupted by the terms, I totally deny. Our author, I ſuppoſe, reads only the Newſpapers, to know what France is now: if he had read Peltier (partial as he is) he muſt have ſeen that neither

poetry

poetry nor philoſophy are on the decline. Some of the writers in the charming Society of the *Vaudeville* are equal in gaiety, elegance, and playfulneſs of humour, to any thing produced in the beſt times of France; and in graver compoſitions, *Le Gouve* and *Vigee* might be a credit to any age or country; the latter ſtrongly reſembles Boileau, and though he has more boldneſs, he appears to have imitated him:* but he deſpiſes every thing that is

* In addition to what I have already ſaid of France, I will here remark, that the events of the war having now nearly driven the French back to their own country, the poſture of affairs is materially changed, and different hopes and expectations are now to be formed: to each party there is but one line of conduct left which wiſdom and honeſty can dictate; but, alas! they ſeldom direct the affairs of the world.—Should the Allies, after having forced the French within their ancient limits, propoſe to them ſuch a peace as might prevent them again from diſturbing the tranquillity of Europe; in caſe of a refuſal, they will be heartily ſupported by all their ſubjects, and ſucceſsfully terminate by the ſword, what negociation failed to accompliſh: or ſhould the French, after having ſucceſsfully defended their country from invaſion, propoſe, to the nations leagued againſt them, ſuch terms of peace as may preſerve their own territory entire, and prevent their interfering with others, they will exhibit an inſtance of magnanimity and prudence which will make it difficult for any government to refuſe their offers; and if after that they ſhould give to other nations the example of a good government,

is French too much to look at it, and yet will give his opinion of what he takes no pains to

vernment, on republican principles, they will do more to propagate thoſe principles than by all the efforts of the ſword: they will exhibit to the eyes and the feelings of ſurrounding nations, arguments which no force of eloquence or of arms can reſiſt: till then, thoſe nations are juſtified in reſiſting the experiment of what they deem uncertain ſpeculations, tho' they are not juſtified in uſing the means they have done to prevent their ſucceſs; but however ſuch an iſſue is to be wiſhed, for the ſake of truth, juſtice, and humanity, it is much to be apprehended that none of theſe will have ſufficient weight; for as all great changes of opinion in the world have occaſioned great convulſions, it is to be feared, that all nations have yet much to ſuffer before the preſent conflict of opinions is terminated. It is more than probable that the different powers at war will contend for a great length of time, with various and alternate ſucceſs: as to what will be the event of the conteſt, there can be little doubt; whether that will ultimately produce good, yet remains to be proved. Let it be remarked, that I here and at all times ſeparate French principles and French conduct: the principles of their conſtitution are excellent; the conduct of their rulers is execrable: they have been connected merely by accident; war is the element of the one, but peace of the other. That any thing ſo intrinſically good ſhould accidentally be connected with evil, is ſomewhat ſtrange, yet it has ever been ſo; and to what wiſe diſpenſation of things it is owing that the beſt gifts of Providence, even Monarchy and Chriſtianity, ſhould have occaſioned ſuch infinite bloodſhed and diſtreſs, it is impoſſible for finite wiſdom to diſcover; it is enough, however, to convince us, that no good can

to be informed in. His quotation from Horace is a happy ſpecimen of his miſrepreſentation: he has made him ſay the exact contrary to what he has ſaid in his Epiſtle to Auguſtus, lines 158 and 159: his words are '*Grave virus munditiæ pepulere.*'—This is to make a man ſay one thing when he means another, and then call it quoting his ſentiments.

" When I name Dryden, I comprehend " every varied excellence of *our* poetry."—Our Author's next praiſe is beſtowed on Dryden, the hireling advocate of any cauſe, the ſucceſſive flatterer of Cromwell and Charles. Surely Pope had many excellencies which Dryden never poſſeſſed; and our Author thinks ſo, for he tells us afterwards that he completed what was wanting in him As to what he calls the *Allegory of Satire*, ſee Johnſon's Life of Dryden, for his opinion of the poem which is ſo highly praiſed. Will the Author be kind enough to explain how this celebrated poem is in any ſhape allegorical: an allegory is a repreſentation of mental qua-

l i es

can be obtained without the expence of much evil, and to make us reſigned to that power, whatever it is, that directs the affairs of the world.

lities or operations, and human actions, under the form of perſonal beings; but Dryden's poem is a repreſentation of modern characters under the names of antient ones: where is there any ſimilarity? to me the things appear very different.

"His ſatire had an original character. It "was the ſtrain of Archilochus ſounding "the lyre of Alcæus." He had neither the virulence of Archilochus, nor the ſweetneſs of Alcæus. The Author, in various parts of his book, takes great pains to have it believed that the ſupport of virtue and morality is one great object of his ſatire, and undoubtedly they are much connected with the literary productions of the times; but they depend not on them ſolely; ſo that when he has reproved the principles of one ſet of men, even ſuppoſing them to be erroneous, he has done but a part of his duty: it was not thus that the great ſatiriſts of antiquity dealt with the times; they reproved vicious characters as well as erroneous principles; and it is thus that every man muſt do who wiſhes to reform:—he muſt be impartial too,—he muſt ſtrike at venality, perfidy, and profligacy, wherever they are to be found,

found,—he muſt enter the palaces of the great, as well as the garrets of the poor, and drag forth titled infamy to ſhame and contempt; and if example is the ſoul of virtue, he muſt endeavour to purify the great,—he muſt chaſtiſe ariſtocratical vices, and pull down ſpiritual wickedneſs in high places; but if he is afraid of Attorney Generals and Treaſury Solicitors, let him no more boaſt of his zeal for religion and morality,—his zeal is only for his employers. In his character of Pope, his language is more than uſually affected: he cannot ſpeak at all as other people do.

"He had excelled in deſcription, in paſ-"toral, in pathetick, and in general criticiſm; "and had given an Engliſh exiſtence in per-"petuity to the Father of all poetry. Thus "honoured, and with theſe pretenſions, he "left them all for that excellence, for which "the maturity of his talents and judgment "ſo eminently deſigned him." I am at a loſs to perceive, how having written paſtoral poetry is to qualify a man for being a ſatiriſt. As to Pope's general criticiſm, the juſtneſs of his precepts in his critical works has been ably diſputed by Dr Aiken, in his Letters to his Son. ‘ He had given an English existence in perpetuity to the Father of all Poetry,’ means, I suppose, that he had translated Homer. ‘ Thus honoured.’ How honoured, he has not told us. If Pope and his writings were not above our Author’s censure, he had never had his praise: he was too free, too liberal a writer, to please him.

“ His works are so generally read and stu-“ died, that I should not merely fatigue, but “ I should almost insult you by such a needless “ disquisition.” This sentence is defective: it wants some member; instead of ‘ *such a needless disquisition,*’ he should have said, ‘ *by a needless disquisition on them.*’

“ As a disciple of these great masters, “ and full of that spirit which an unbroken “ and an honourable intimacy with their “ works has inspired, I now present myself a “ votary at their temple; and in some mea-“ sure clothed in the robes of their heredita-“ ry priesthood, I would also enter, and offer “ my oblation at the high altar of my “ country. But if, unworthy of this hallow-“ ed investment and interior ministry, the “ door of the sanctuary is closed upon me; “ I shall retire without a murmur, and, with “ devotion

" devotion unimpaired, worſhip in the veſ- " tibule." Here is confuſion worſe confounded. He is a miniſter in the temple of ſatire, if any body ever heard of ſuch a temple, and yet he offers his oblations on the high altar of his country: he is at once the votary and the prieſt, and yet he doubts whether he is worthy of the ſacred inveſtment. To be in ſome meaſure clothed, is to be little better than naked; and I doubt ſome people will ſay this is our Author's caſe, as far as regards his poetical garments: but after all, his modeſty ſteps in, and, though ſtripped of his holy robes, and kicked out of the temple, he is determined to pray in the porch. I am ſorry to ſay he deſerves no better place; but this comes of being preſumptuous. The quotation at the end is partly from Statius and partly of his own making: *vide* Statius, lib. 4. 4. l. 54. where it will be ſeen how much belongs to each of the two.

Having now gone over the particulars of that part of his work which I have undertaken at preſent to examine, it becomes me to review the ſubſtance of what he has advanced, for the purpoſe of obviating more fully the effect of his doctrines. To ſay much of his politics might not now be ſafe ; for the ſide he has choſen is protected by the ſtrong arm of power, ready to fall on all thoſe who differ from him. I will therefore only ſay, in general, that he ſeems to have no liberal or comprehenſive idea of government and ſociety ; of the means by which they have arrived at their preſent excellence, or the poſſibility of further improvement : whatever is eſtabliſhed, is, with him, conſecrated from the rude touch of innovation ; and even the gentle progreſs of time can work no change for the better, as if the world was not a continued ſcene of change, and the experience of ages did not teach us that principles and cuſtoms, the moſt abhorrent from the ideas of one race of men, become familiar and eaſy to others. According to his maxims, hiſtory and philoſophy have nothing more to teach us ; and the world, inſtead of being henceforth what it has hitherto been, (a ſeries of experiments) is now arrived at ſuch a pitch of excellence in politics, religion, and morality, as precludes the poſſibility of any further lights,—we muſt ſit down ſatisfied with what we are, and teach our children to do the ſame, or be called Jacobins, and treated as ſuch

ſuch,—we muſt acquieſce with our author and his friends * in the belief of what they tell us,—we muſt read only ſuch books as they allow us,—we muſt approve what they approve, or be condemned as diſturbers of the public peace, and enemies of all eſtabliſhed government: ſuch is his liberality, and ſuch his exertions for the good of mankind. He may mean well, but he is certainly miſtaken, for the teſtimony of all ages is againſt him. Mankind never were the ſame in their laws, their religion, or their cuſtoms, for a hundred years together in any civilized country upon earth: even maxims that have been conſidered as fundamental, have yielded to the force of time, much leſs the fleeting forms of political eſtabliſhments. To hate and perſecute their enemies, was the religion and the policy of the Jews; to love them, was the milder precept of Chriſtianity: hiſtory is but the record of perpetual change, and the analogy of nature confirms the exiſtence of the propenſity in man: what was land once is now ſea: earthquakes and volcanoes have ſwept away cities, and the habitations of men are now inhabited by beaſts: the ſeat of empire, arts, and commerce,

* The authors of the Anti-Jacobin and their employers.

merce, has been perpetually changing, and is now transferred from the eastern to the western continent; and, with all this change, the world is without doubt, on the whole, improved: yet the vanity and arrogance of one little mortal has possessed him with the belief that he can arrest the progress of nature and of man, and make that stationary which Providence has hitherto made progressive. Vain mortal! check thy presumptuous folly, and learn to believe that it is not for thee, nor for all those who are the idols of thy worship, to restrain the innate propensities of thy species, to set thy seal upon the door of wisdom, nor to say to the soul of man, in the search after truth, '*Thus far shalt thou go, and no farther.*

The next leading feature in his introductory letter is his severe condemnation of all freethinkers in religion, for which I will only suggest to him the possibility of his being mistaken in what he believes to be right, from the example of men who were thought to be wiser than him having embraced as truth what we now consider as error. More and Erasmus were Papists, and believed doctrines which our author, by the help of the superior lights

lights which have been acquired ſince their times, now very wiſely conſiders as ridiculous: it may be his fate to have ſome of his opinions thought as ridiculous by poſterity.

Another ſtrong part of his letter is his zeal againſt Popery; a zeal which I have endeavoured to direct to its proper object, and to ſhew our Author where the true ground of fear exiſts: he has been very violent againſt the emigrants who have fled, and the Papiſts who are tolerated here; but it is not of them that I have any dread; they do not alarm me: if I have any fear, it is from the popery of proteſtant divines, not of French emigrants,—the popery of a church which is rich and eſtabliſhed, not of one which is in poverty and exile: it is from the doctrines of ſpiritual power and civil ſubmiſſion, now preached by the aſpiring miniſters of a church which can reward their ambition, and a government which courts their ſervices, not from the impotent and unambitious miniſters of a ſect which has no longer either power or influence; whoſe doctrines are diſregarded becauſe they are unſupported by authority, and whoſe only object is to obtain protection, not power: the Whore of Babylon has loſt

all

all her wealth and attractions, but her daughter is yet rich and admired. His frequent quotations, of which he attempts a defence, I have ſtrongly reprobated; he is appriſed of his failing, and endeavours to obviate it, by tranſlations of the paſſages he has quoted, yet not without contradicting his own opinions;* for he has laid great ſtreſs on the utility of the original words of claſſical authors, to enforce and illuſtrate what he has advanced. I will hereafter ſhew that his tranſlations are not faithful, and have conſiderably weakened the force and effect of the authors he has quoted, and that if he underſtood them, he was determined other people ſhould not.

The faults of his critical principles will be more fully ſhewn when I have occaſion to remark them in different parts of his writings in which he has cenſured the works of others. His ſtile, if examined by any of the rules of legitimate compoſition, will be found to contain all the faults, and few of the beauties, that have been noticed by the greateſt critics: it is frigid, affected, harſh, bombaſtical and puerile; it is metaphorical, but his meta-

* *Vide* page 26.

metaphors are far ſought, and ill adapted; it is poetical without being harmonious; it has the uncouthneſs without the force of antiquity; it is not always intelligible, ſometimes not grammatical, and conſtantly the reverſe of ſimplicity and purity: if any man wiſhes to ſee ſome of its faults more forcibly and neatly expreſſed than it is in my power to expreſs, I will refer him to Dionyſius's enumeration of the faults of Plato's ſtile, which are numerous: *Vide* Dionyſius's Epiſt. ad Cn. Pomp. Ed Sylb 1586. p. 127. l. 20. ſect. 5. and to the ſame author's judgment of others who affected a poetical and pompous phraſeology, *vide* Dionyſius Lyſias, line 27.

His ideas on the chief ſatiriſts of ancient and modern time, I truſt, I have ſhewn to be defective and erroneous, in not having mentioned all that deſerve the praiſe of excellence, and in having given a falſe account of thoſe whom he has mentioned; but, on the whole, to ſpeak impartially of his talents and his acquirements, I will confeſs, that he has ſometimes a rare felicity of expreſſion; that he is moderately verſed in claſſical learning, but deſtitute of invention and judgment; that his philological information is various and extenſive, but not accurate ; that he is better ſuited to the detail of parts than to comprehend or to create a ſyſtem ; that his ſtile is ſometimes rich, but always laboured ; that his powers are much indebted to cultivation, but partake very little of genius ; and that, with ſome juſt ſentiments of religion, he wants the vital principle of Chriſtianity.

I have now nearly finiſhed, for the preſent, with this contemptible Author, and, if I have failed to expoſe his arrogance, ignorance, and wickedneſs, I will yet add a few words more, without fear of repetition, for he has afforded abundant matter, ſuch as it is, for reiterated cenſure. Had he been what he pretends to be, (a legitimate ſucceſſor of the great ſatiriſts of former times) I ſhould never have preſumed nor deſired to reprove him,—had he, like them, ſhewn a generous indignation againſt vice, without any tincture of private or party malignity,—had he poſſeſſed their compact and regular ſtile of writing, without wandering into needleſs excurſions,—had he, either in poetry or in proſe, ſhewn the virtues of a great ſoul or the talents of a great genius, I ſhould never have dared to lift my feeble voice againſt ſuch powers,

pro-

properly direćted: had his ſtile been any thing but a tiſſue of quotations, even where they are not acknowledged,—had he been uniformly low, in ſtile and ideas, I ſhould have ſuffered him to paſs quietly by unnoticed and unmoleſted; but when I ſee an author without one ſpark of the heavenly ſire of genius, without one generous or liberal principle, with a ſanguinary thirſt for perſecution and a virulent intolerance of all difference of opinion, a rooted prejudice for the eſtabliſhments of Chriſtianity, without one particle of its ſpirit,—when I ſee an author, whoſe only greatneſs conſiſts in his own conſequence, impoſing upon the public, with the air of independence and dignity,—when I ſee an author whoſe only merit as a ſcholar is that of having read the claſſics, without being improved by them, perpetually recalling us to the ancient models of compoſition, while he is perpetually violating them; a man who has ſacrificed the purity and ſimplicity of his native language to the affećtation of novelty and the affećtation of knowledge,—when I ſee ſuch a man taking advantage of the times, and labouring to depreſs the beſt men, and the beſt principles, without one requisite for a satirist but his virulence, imposing upon the taste and pockets of the public, by a perpetual repetition of his malignant effusions, under the cover of darkness shooting his poisoned arrows at the peace of the community, and slandering in secret those whom he dare not face openly; sowing the seeds of jealousy, suspicion, and distrust among men, by concealing his name, and yet condemning with merciless severity the foibles of others,—when I see such a man receive the slightest countenance, I feel an indignation at his impudence and the public infatuation, which no considerations of danger can repress. I feel for the national character when I see it degraded by listening to the dark suggestions of an anonymous incendiary,—I feel for the dignity of classical learning, when it is prostituted to so vile a purpose,—I feel for the injured names of those men, from whose writings I first imbibed the glorious sentiments of liberty, when they are called in to sanction the most daring encroachments on the birth-right of Britons, and lend a force to the denunciations of a sanguinary bigot,—I feel for the condition of posterity, when I see the Author of the

the Purſuits of Literature ſet up for a guide of the public taſte, a guardian of the public morals, and a defender of the public liberty; and if I have ſpoken with more than uſual warmth, I am urged by that ſpirit of liberty and truth which yields to no temptation, and requires no reſtraint.

Morpeth, May 22, 1799.

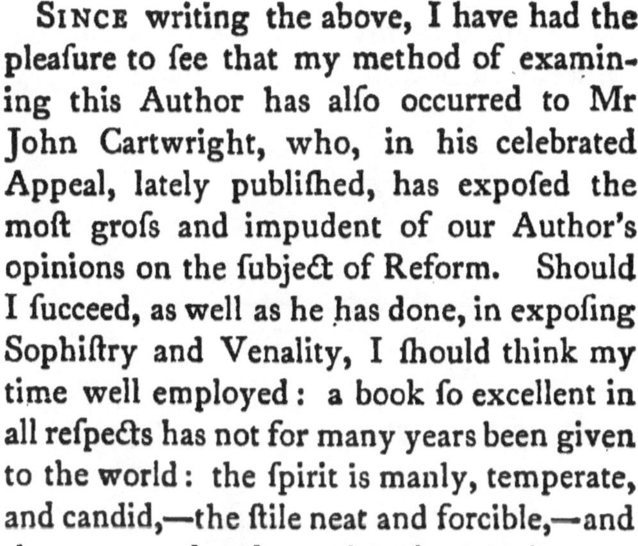

SINCE writing the above, I have had the pleaſure to ſee that my method of examining this Author has alſo occurred to Mr John Cartwright, who, in his celebrated Appeal, lately publiſhed, has expoſed the moſt groſs and impudent of our Author's opinions on the ſubject of Reform. Should I ſucceed, as well as he has done, in expoſing Sophiſtry and Venality, I ſhould think my time well employed: a book ſo excellent in all reſpects has not for many years been given to the world: the ſpirit is manly, temperate, and candid,—the ſtile neat and forcible,—and the matter abundant; but it contains too much truth not to be proſecuted: the manner

ner in which it is delivered to the public, ſhews, however, that the Author is firmly prepared for the worſt.—In addition to what I have already remarked, I muſt here notice what I had omitted before,—that the words (page 32.) ‘ Quos orbe ſub omni Jam vix ‘ ſeptena numerat Sapientia fama,’ are not marked as belonging to any author, nor do I immediately recollect from whom they are quoted. I have omitted other things, perhaps of more conſequence, but I truſt that my preſent diſtance from the converſation of literary men, and my reſidence in a diſtant province, will be admitted as my apology.

FINIS.

Printed by M. Brown, Fleſh-Market, Newcaſtle upon Tyne.

www.ingramcontent.com/pod-product-compliance
Lightning Source LLC
Chambersburg PA
CBHW032200010726
47493CB00008BA/2773

* 9 7 8 3 3 3 7 2 0 3 2 0 7 *